The Village Fête

A play

Peter Tinniswood

Samuel French — London
New York - Toronto - Hollywood

CHARACTERS

Nancy
Father
Rosie
William
Winston
Mrs Godwin
Stanley
Janet

The action of the play takes place in the London and the country homes of the Empson family

Time: the present

The Village Fête has also appeared, in different forms, as a radio play and as a novel under the title *Hayballs*. The characters in *The Village Fête* have also appeared in the continuing radio series *Winston* and in the novel *Winston*.

———————————

Also by Peter Tinniswood, published by Samuel French Ltd:

You Should See Us Now

ACT I

The empty drawing room of the house in London. Packing cases and black plastic sacks

Nancy Empson, a handsome woman in her early to mid forties, is brushing the bare floor. Her brother, William, in his early thirties, sits sulkily in a packing case, legs dangling. Her sister, Rosie, in her mid twenties, stares out of the window

Silently, two Removal Men trudge across the stage, carrying a rusty old lawn mower and an assortment of gardening implements

Nancy The house spider's done a bunk.
　　　He's gone AWOL.
　　　Spider, spider! Where are you, spider?
　　　Come and see us before we go.
　　　Come and say bye bye. Spider, spider.

The two Removal Men trudge back for more implements

William It's all so outrageously inconvenient.
Rosie Moving house is always inconvenient, William.
William But it's specifically inconvenient to me, Rosie.
　　　I am approaching the denouement of my book.
　　　It's all locked away in my head.
　　　I am rapidly approaching the denouement.
　　　Do you understand—the denouement.
　　　And this move will absolutely destroy it.
Rosie How can anyone possibly have a denouement in a book about the
　　Dorset and Somerset Railway?
William It is not the Dorset and Somerset Railway.
　　　Quite the reverse, in fact.
　　　It is the Somerset and Dorset Railways.

In the plural.

Rosie Oh, I'm so sorry, William.

That makes all the difference, doesn't it?

William Oh, you can sneer. You can mock.

But if it weren't for these books of mine, which you dismiss so contemptuously, a major part of the income of this household would be lost forever.

And then where should we be?

Rosie Ah yes. The old story.

Now let me see.

It was the Hull and Barnsley Railway which paid for the new fridge-freezer.

It was the Cambrian Coast Line which bought us the new bathroom suite in crushed avocado.

It was the...

William My God, why did I ever stick with this family?

I could have lived on my own and wallowed in the fame and esteem I never remotely sniff in this bloody household.

Rosie You get esteem, William.

You get esteem.

You drag it out of us, screaming and kicking.

You are the most thoroughly spoiled man I have ever met in the whole of my life.

William Me? Spoiled?

Rosie Yes.

William Well, if being spoiled is allowing myself to be dragged away from my roots here in London where I'm happy to vegetate in the Godforsaken countryside, then you've got a very funny idea of the meaning of the word.

Rosie There's no need for you to come with us.

Stay.

William You know perfectly well I can't stay.

Rosie Why?

William Well ... well ... you know why.

Rosie No, I don't, William.

You're a very self-contained man.

A loner.

You prefer your own company.

That's what you're always telling us, isn't it?

William Yes.

Rosie So stay here and fend for yourself.

I'd have thought you'd manage very well.

A nice little bedsitter in Belsize Park, maybe.

You know—tatty velvet curtains and a threadbare Indian carpet and one of those gas rings hidden away in a fitted wardrobe.

And a landlady who slip slops round the house with a cigarette permanently stuck to her lower lip.

And cat hairs and the smell of cabbage and...

You'd love it, William. You'd adore it.

William You know perfectly well it would kill me.

Rosie That's why you've got to move with us, then, isn't it, William?

William Father's chest.

Why have we always got to move because of Father?

Father's chest. Father's legs. Father's headaches. Father's...

Rosie We move because we love Father.

William Oh, do we?

Rosie Yes, we do.

William I don't.

At this moment I do not love Father.

Rosie Yes, you do.

William No, I don't.

Rosie You do, you do, you do.

Nancy (*to the audience*) We are what is called A Happy Family.

A talented family.

My brother, William, is an author.

My sister, Rosie, is a designer of textiles.

My father, before his retirement, was the headmaster of a most prestigious private school with its own carp pond.

And my talent?

(*She laughs bitterly*) My talent is in keeping us all together.

Pause

Spider, spider!

Where are you, spider?

Rosie He's gone, Nancy.

He's deserted us.

He doesn't want to know us now.

William Neither do I.
Nancy I'm going in the garden to look for Father.

> I hope he hasn't set his trousers alight with his pipe again.

She goes into the garden

> Father, Father.
> Where are you, Father?

Father is a dapper man in his early seventies

Father Over here, Nancy.
Nancy Father! (*She kisses him on his forehead*) You smell of foot powder.
Father I can hear a thrush singing.
Nancy I know.
Father I like the sound of thrushes.
Nancy You'll hear lots and lots of thrushes in the country, Father.
Father I know.

> But I shall miss the city thrushes.
> Fearfully pleasant coves, city thrushes.

A jumbo jet is heard passing low overhead

> I shall miss the jumbo jets, too, Nancy.

Nancy No, you won't, Father.
Father Yes, I will.

> I used to like watching them passing overhead and wondering where
> they were going to.
> Peru, Sarawak, the Trucial States.
> The sky's the limit, eh?

Nancy Come along, Father.

> It's time to go.

Father Yes.

> Yes, another house to say farewell to.

Nancy We're getting quite expert at it, aren't we, Father?
Father Yes.

> It's my chest, you see.
> I need the fresh air of the country.
> I need the smell of bullocks and fresh dung.

Nancy Of course you do, Father.

Father You see, Nancy, when we lived by the sea it was my sinuses that couldn't cope.

Fearful set of bastards, my sinuses.

And my knees aren't behind the door when it comes to making a thorough-going nuisance of themselves.

Nancy I know, Father, I know.

Come along.

Say bye bye to the thrush.

Father Bye bye, thrush.

Your singing's been absolutely tip top.

Couldn't fault it.

Well done, old chap.

Nancy (*gently*) Come on.

She leads him into the drawing room

Father What-ho, Rosie.

Has the house spider put in an appearance yet?

Rosie Yes, Father, yes.

He just came out now and...

William And the removal men squashed him to pulp.

Squelch, it went. Yooook.

Rosie William!

William Well.

Nancy Now come on, you two.

Let's leave this house with dignity, shall we?

Let's leave it in tranquillity.

Let's leave it with nothing but happy memories of us. Yes?

Father Time for the off then, is it?

Has the Volvo decided which way it's taking us?

Nancy I've decided, Father.

We'll go by the M4.

William I hate motorways.

Rosie You hate everything today, William.

William That is not true, Rosie.

My hatred for motorways is long-established and well-known in the family.

Look at all the traffic they create—juggernauts, coaches, petrol

tankers, ghastly Spaniards with hairy chests and dirty teeth driving
refrigerated lorries full of heroin and boot-leg brandy.

Now if we only transferred them all to rail, we'd have a well-
organised, well-integrated, rationalized transport system.

I've said it time and time again in my books.

I've written umpteen articles in newspapers and magazines and...

Why are you tugging at my sleeve, Father?

Father I want to tell you something.

William What?

Father I used to like travelling by rail.

Rosie Did you, Father?

Father Ra-ther.

I once made a trip across India by rail.

With your mother.

When she was alive.

Rosie How exciting, Father.

Father Yes, it was.

I can't remember a thing about it.

Except that it was exciting. Fearfully exciting.

Yes.

We ate a lot of curry, if my memory serves me correct.

William I quite like curry.

Father You take after your mother.

She liked curry when she was alive.

Nancy We all like curry, Father.

Rosie I don't.

William Well, that's news to me.

You always used to like it.

Rosie I don't like it now.

William Rubbish.

Rosie It is not rubbish.

I do not like curry now, and if I am challenged any more on the
subject, I shall go screaming mad.

Nancy That's enough, Rosie. Enough.

I've got over a hundred miles of driving ahead of me.

I have to concentrate. I have to have peace.

I do not wish to be distracted by my family squabbling and shouting
and screaming.

So calm it.

Calm down.

Calm down, everyone, shall we?

Rosie (*icily*) Yes, Nancy. Anything you say, Nancy.

But of course, Nancy.

Nancy Good.

How sweet of you. How thoughtful.

(*Briskly*) Right, everyone. Batten down the emotions. Stiffen the lips. Straighten the shoulders. And off we go. No looking back. No dawdling. No wallowing in memories.

Time to leave.

She claps her hands and ushers them off

Only Father remains

Father Well, bye bye, old chap. Farewell.

It's not my fault we're leaving you, you know.

It's my chest. Or is it my lungs?

I can't remember.

Fearful brutes, the bodily functions, aren't they?

So ungrateful to all the hard work you put in trying to keep them in good nick.

Kidneys, liver, heart, colon, lower gut—they're all the same.

Absolute bastards.

You spend a lifetime cosseting them and pampering them and going to endless trouble and inconvenience keeping them happy and then what happens?

The swines turn round on you and without a word of gratitude boot you into touch.

"Sorry, old boy," they say. "We've had enough. We're packing up. We're calling it a day."

Well, thanks very much, you stinkers. Where does that leave me?

Typical of the modern world. People just don't want to see a job through to the bitter end, do they?

My bloody chest.

My blasted sinuses. My lungs, my liver.

I've a good mind to have them thoroughly horse-whipped.

(*He pauses*) Well then, goodbye, house.

Don't blame me.

It wasn't my fault.

He exits slowly

Black-out

Lights up to reveal the garden of the new house

Nancy, William, Rosie, and Father are standing outside

Nancy Well then, everyone.
   Our new house.
   What do you think?
William It looks extremely damp to me.
Rosie And extremely malevolent and extremely uncooperative.
Nancy Don't talk such nonsense, Rosie.
   It's a lovely house.
   It's got a nice smile to it. A cheery face. A happy, loving counte-
   nance.

Roar of a helicopter passing overhead

Father And it's got helicopters, too.
Nancy Of course it has, Father.
   And that's why I know you're going to simply adore it here.
Father They're army helicopters, Nancy.
   Full of chaps. I like things that are full of chaps. That's why I got on
   so well with India.
   Positively bursting with chaps, India, you know.
   Did I ever tell you about that chap I knew in Bombay who used to
   import cough lozenges and vaulting horses?
William Yes, you did, Father.
   And he lived in Madras.
Father So he did. He lived in Madras.
   That's typical of the sort of thing chaps get up to in India, you know.
   (*He smiles*) Yes, I'm going to like this place—provided my legs hold
   out, of course.
Rosie (*icily*) But of course, Father.
   Of course.

Nancy Well then, chaps.

There's no point hanging round here like a band of refugees.

Shall we go in?

But of course we will, Nancy.

After you, Nancy.

Right then. This way. Follow me.

She leads them inside

So what do you think?

Rosie I can smell gas.

William So can I.

Nancy (*sniffing hard*) Good grief. You're right.

Put your pipe out, Father.

Father Pardon?

Nancy Your pipe, Father.

Put it out.

There's a smell of gas.

Father I can't smell a thing, old boy.

It's my sinuses, you see.

The bastards have decided to pack up on me again.

I won't have it, you know. I'll...

Rosie Ring the emergency service, William.

William What?

Rosie Ring the emergency service.

William But how will I know its number?

Nancy Look in the phone book, William.

It'll be under...

Oh, never mind. I'll do it.

And put out that pipe, Father.

You'll blow us all to smithereens.

Father Oh, lord, we wouldn't want that, would we?

Frightfully inconvenient.

I once saw a naval monitor blown to smithereens on the Hooghly River.

Made a fearful mess of the chaps.

Nancy (*to the audience*) The emergency men came and discovered that we had a twenty-two per cent gas leak.

And it was rising.

So they cut off our gas.

And so we had no cooking and no heating.

And in the middle of all this while they were digging up the road outside the house to find the mains the removal men arrived.

Removal Men enter, carrying objects

William Mind what you're doing with that cabinet.

For God's sake, be careful.

The drawers are still full.

All my notes on the Somerset and Dorset are in there.

Be careful.

Rosie And be careful with my table.

That is an antique table. It's priceless.

Good Lord, you're ripping it to bits.

Nancy Please, Rosie, please, William.

Calm down. Calm down.

Everything's going to be all right.

Father enters

Father Well, there's nothing wrong with the ablutions facilities.

Nancy What?

Father The old ablutions, Nancy.

Fearfully pleasant flush it's got.

Charming noise it makes.

Seems to be saying "Thanks very much for using me. Come again some time."

And I will, too, old boy. I'll make a point of it.

And I'll tell you something else, too.

Nancy What's that, Father?

Father I've discovered a shed at the bottom of the garden.

Nancy Have you really?

Father Yes.

It'll be absolutely perfect for smoking my pipe in.

Rosie (*tartly*) Oh. Good.

I'm so pleased for you, Father. We're all pleased.

Father How kind of you to say so, Rosie.

How agreeable.

Well then, I think I'll potter off back there.

Have a pipe—or something rather like it.
Don't want me here with all these gas wallahs, do you?
Never was very good with gas.
Or with electricity, if it comes to that.
Always was absolutely useless round the house.
That's what your mother used to say when she was alive.
When she was alive she used to say to me:
"You're absolutely useless round the house."
And I was.
Absolutely useless. A complete duffer.

He potters off

Nancy (*to the audience*) And then the emergency men condemned the
    boiler.
    They said we had to have a new one.
    They put a notice on the old boiler.
    It said "Condemned."
    I felt so sorry for the poor little thing crouching there all forlorn like
    a dog you're taking to the vets to be put down.
    I wanted to cuddle it.
Rosie How long before we get a new one?
Nancy About three or four weeks they said.
Rosie Oh, charming. Oh, whoopee.
William I hate today.
    I hate it, hate it, hate it.
Nancy (*half to herself*) Poor you.
    What would you do without me?
    How could you possibly survive?

Ring on the doorbell

William Who's that?
Rosie What a stupid thing to say, William.
    How can we possibly know who it is until we answer the door?
    Do you think I've got X-ray eyes?
    Do you think I've——
Nancy I'll go, Rosie.
    I'll go.
    (*On her way to the front door*) Leave it to Nancy. As usual.

Good old Nancy.
(*She goes to the front door*)

Stanley and Janet are standing there. They're in their mid forties

Yes?

Stanley (*startled*) Ah. Yes.

Yes, well, we're your new neighbours.

We've come about the village fête.

Nancy Sorry?

Stanley May we come in?

Nancy Of course.

How rude of me.

I do hope you'll excuse the mess.

Stanley Certainly.

May I introduce my wife?

This is my wife.

Her name's Janet.

Janet How do you do?

My name's Janet.

Nancy Yes.

Well, my name's Nancy.

Nancy Empson.

Stanley Empson? Empson?

I know that name.

It's most unusual, isn't it?

Nancy It is quite.

Stanley My name's Jones.

That's not an unusual name. It's Welsh actually—in origin.

Janet But we're not Welsh.

Nancy Ah.

Janet We're English.

Nancy Good. Splendid. It's nice to be among fellow nationals, isn't it?

Well, perhaps you'd like to come into the drawing room and I could offer you something.

Stanley No, no. We don't want to intrude.

It's just that we thought we'd come about the village fête.

Nancy The village fête?

Stanley That's right.

It's at the end of the month.

We all take part in the village fête.

Well, it's expected from this end of the village.

We all run a stall, and we thought you'd like to decide which stall you want to run.

Nancy Yes, but it's rather inconvenient at the moment.

We've had a twenty-two per cent gas leak.

They've cut us off and condemned our boiler.

We haven't started to unpack yet.

So ... so it's rather inconvenient, you see.

Stanley I suppose it must be.

Janet Moving into strange houses is always inconvenient, isn't it?

That's why Stanley and I don't move.

It's a matter of principle, isn't it, Stanley?

Stanley Quite right, Janet.

We are what I like to call "stay-putters".

We've lived in this village for...

Empson? Empson? Got it.

Isn't it to do with writing?

Isn't there a famous writer called Empson?

Nancy Well, there's the famous poet, William Empson.

Stanley William Empson! That's it.

But he's not a poet. He writes books about railways.

Are you by any chance related to him?

Nancy Yes.

William is my brother.

Stanley Good gracious me. How wonderful.

I am a train buff myself, you know.

Nancy Really?

Stanley Oh yes. I've got a library full of books about railways.

I've got every book that's ever been written by William Empson, haven't I, Janet?

Janet You certainly have, Stanley.

And they're real dust hoarders, too.

Not just his books. Everybody's books.

I wouldn't want to single him out.

Stanley I should say not.

William Empson! I would go so far as to say that he's quite a hero of mine.

Nancy In that case come and meet him.

Stanley He's ... he's in this house? Now?

Nancy Oh yes. Permanently. He'll be living here.
Stanley Good gracious me. What luck.
        This is the happiest day of my life.
Nancy Jolly good. Let's try and make it ecstatic, shall we? Follow me.

She leads them into the drawing room

        William, Rosie. These are our new neighbours, Stanley and Janet.

They murmur greetings. Stanley goes up to William and pounds his hand

Stanley Actually, I'm the Stanley half of the duo.
William Good.
Stanley I must say I'm a terrific fan of yours.
        I think the book I most admired of yours, William ... if I may call you
        William, of course.
William Yes, you may.
Stanley Thank you.
        I think the book I most admired of yours was that lovely little slim
        volume about the branch lines of the South Wales Coalfield.
William Ah yes.
        That was always a favourite of mine.
Stanley Mind you, I'd be hard-pressed to set it before your marvellous
        history of the London and North Western Railway.
William Yes.
        A great favourite of mine, the London and North Western Railway.
Stanley Mine too. Didn't they have the most wonderful locomotives?
        I'm a particular fan of the George the Fifth class, four-four-o.
William Ah yes. Splendid engines. They'd got Schmidt superheaters, you
        know.
Stanley Oh, I know, I know.
Janet He knows everything about railways, does Stanley.
        He's particularly good on couplings.
Rosie Really? You could have fooled me.
Nancy (*hastily*) Yes, well, perhaps Janet's got some useful tips she can
        pass on now we're living in the country.
Janet Oh, certainly.
        The first thing you've got to remember is that we don't get the
        services here you city slickers get in the city.
Rosie We're hardly city slickers.

Janet Yes, I know.

But you obviously expect to be able to pick up the phone and everyone will come rushing out to you.

You want this attended to, you want that attended to, and out they come at the drop of a hat.

Well, they don't here.

Nancy What do they do, Janet?

What do you do, if anything goes wrong?

Janet Oh, simple. We ring for Winston.

Rosie Winston?

Janet Yes, he's the local odd job man and poacher.

If you want any plumbing done, you call for Winston.

If you want a tree chopped down, you call for Winston.

If you want a brace of pheasant or new castors for your cocktail cabinet, you call for Winston.

He's absolutely invaluable, is Winston.

We couldn't survive without him.

Rosie Then we'd better call up Winston, hadn't we?

Black-out

Lights up on Nancy in a working smock

Nancy (*to the audience*) And so I called up Winston.

He arrived at our house three days later.

Three days in which half the ceiling in the drawing room fell down, in which we discovered half the sockets and switches in the house were live, in which we discovered the most disgusting smell in the downstairs loo, in which we... (*She laughs a bitter little laugh*) in which we discovered everything.

Ring on the doorbell. She opens the door

Winston is standing there

Yes?

Winston grins broadly at her. He is a stocky man with a nut brown boozer's belly. His shirt is open to the waist. His hair curls over his shoulders. He has a Zapata moustache. He wears filthy wellingtons rolled down to the ankles. He is in his late thirties

Winston The name's Winston.

Winston Hayballs, poet, poacher, and philosopher.

Admirer of the collected works of Mrs Gaskell as wrote by herself in person and acknowledged expert on stench pipes, out fall pipes and all matters pertaining to the successful functioning of your bogs both inside and out.

Nancy You've got tattoos on your nipples.

Winston Indeed I have, missus. Without a doubt.

Above the right one I got the word "Mild". And above the left one I got the word "Bitter".

Like to see what I got tattooed on my buttocks?

Nancy No, I would not.

Winston In that case I shall content myself by commenting favourably on the shape of your pins and the general handsomeness of your endowments and sundry proclivities.

Nancy I beg your pardon?

He steps inside without being asked and breathes in deeply

Winston Ah yes, he haven't changed, this old house.

Same old smell of hamster droppings and hairy navels.

Nancy What?

Winston I knows this house well, missus.

Oh yes, old Winston, he knows this house like the back of his hand.

Nancy I see.

It has a history, has it?

Winston Course it has, missus. Without a doubt.

And so had its previous and prior owner, old Wilson Rappaport. You ever met him?

Nancy No. He died two months before I came to view the house.

Winston That was the worst thing what you ever done in your life look.

Nancy Pardon?

Winston The worst thing you ever done in your life was to come down here from the city and take over this house from old Wilson Rappaport.

Nancy Why?

Winston (*tapping his nose conspiratorially*) Because of what he was, missus. Because of his intrinsics.

Wilson Rappaport? What a man.

A laugh. A rogue and a vagabond. And a weaver of spells and mysteries.

And he organised the village fête look.

Nancy The village fête?

That's all I've heard since we moved in—the village fête.

Winston Well, you would, missus.

The village fête? It's the highlight of the year here.

And it's being held at the end of the month look.

Nancy Yes, I have been made aware of that.

Winston Good, good.

Just so long as you knows.

Ain't you got a nice smooth neck?

Nancy What?

Winston My current bit of fluff what's concurrent at the moment, she ain't got a smooth white neck.

No. She got a dumpy little neck with jowls and a shaving rash.

Are you going to keep that swimming pool at the back end of your garden?

Nancy I don't think so.

Winston You do right, missus.

That swimming pool, he's a positive death trap, is that swimming pool look.

Full of germs from top to bottom.

Nancy I see.

Winston Course, old Winston Rappaport, well, he looked after it proper.

Oh yes.

He heated it. He filtrated it. Course, he didn't pay for nothing.

Nancy No?

Winston No.

He just by-passed the gas meter.

That's why you got all them pipes littered over your garden look.

No legality to them.

He botched them up hisself personal.

Nancy That probably explains why we had a gas leak.

Twenty-two per cent and rising.

Winston Course it do.

And your electrics'll be up the spout, too.

Nancy That's one of the things I want to see you about.

Winston I knows.

I was waiting for you to call about them.

As soon as I knew new folk was moving in, I said to the missus with her fat legs and mottled shins, I says:

"Won't be long before they call to ask about the electrics," I says.
And your roof needs doing, too.

Nancy Not according to the surveyor.

Winston Oh, you don't want to take no notice of surveyors, missus.
They don't know nothing round here look.
You get a surveyor in the city, and he knows something.
Well, with all them sex shops and massage parlours in Soho, he's
bound to pick up a bit of knowledge, ain't he?
But you get a surveyor here in the country and...
Do you know your extension's illegal?

Nancy Pardon?

Winston The extension at the back of your kitchen—he's illegal.
Old Wilson Rappaport he never got no planning permission for it.

Nancy No?

Winston No. Not him.

Nancy Is it important?

Winston Course it's important, missus.
When you lives in the country, look, you has to get planning
permission for everything.
You has to have planning permission, if you wants to go and have a
shit.

Nancy Thank you very much, Winston, but I don't think we'll have
language like that round this house, if you please.
Now then, perhaps you'd like to have a look round and see what
needs doing and give us an estimate.

Winston Oh, I doesn't need to do that, missus.
Old Winston knows what needs doing look.
See this meter here? Well, he needs slinging straight away.
He's dangerous.
And he's illegal, too.
And look at this rad here.
That's what we calls radiators in the trade look.
Well, he needs throwing out.
They all needs throwing out.
And your roof?
Well, he needs doing as I already said and stated.
And your swimming pool needs going out.
Everything needs going out.
This house, missus, he needs completely re-gutting from top to
bottom.

Nancy I have to tell you, Winston, that it wasn't my plan when we moved here to have the house completely re-gutted.

The survey simply said it needed a certain amount of work doing.

Winston Ah yes, missus, but what did they mean by "a certain amount of work?"

They probably said that after they completed the Leaning Tower of Pisa.

And look at the state of it now.

A bleeding death trap if you tried to fry bacon in it.

No wonder the Eyeties always eats spaghetti.

Ain't you got nice-shaped ears?

Nancy What?

Winston Your ears, missus. The old lug holes. They're a nice shape. Very dainty. Very demure.

Not like the ears on the bit of fluff I had before the one I got now.

Great big danglers she had. Gynormous.

You could have bunged them full of nasturtiums and used them for hanging baskets if you didn't mind being pollinated by bees in the spring.

Nancy I'm not interested in your bits of fluff, Winston.

What I'm interested in is showing you round the house and getting some work done as soon as possible.

Now this is my brother William's study.

(*She calls*) William, is it convenient if we come in for a minute?

William (*from inside the study*) It's never convenient to come in when I'm working.

Nancy But I've got the workman here, William.

He wants to see what needs doing.

William (*from inside the study*) OK, all right. But make it quick.

I'm right in the middle of the section on the marshalling yards at Shepton Mallet.

Get that wrong and I've lost the whole feel and voice of the book.

I've totally...

Oh, come on in.

Winston and Nancy enter the study

Nancy This is Winston.

Winston, this is my brother, William.

Winston How do you do, sir?

Very pleasant to make your acquaintance.

How long have you suffered from that dandruff?

William What?

Winston (*ignoring him completely*) My God, this room.

Cor, he's in a state.

William What do you mean "he's in a state?"

Winston Well, look at your electrics.

They're a death trap.

William What?

Winston They're a death trap.

You put a plug in that socket, and you'll go up like a Trident rocket.

William You mean it's dangerous?

Winston Course he is. Without a doubt.

I takes this screwdriver look and I sticks it in that socket, and what happens? (*He puts a screwdriver in the socket*)

There is a loud bang

Look at that.

If I didn't know what I was doing, I'd have been a gonner now.

Fried alive like a little pile of rabbit tods.

William Oh, my Lord.

Winston Not to worry, William.

I'll soon fix him up for you.

And I'll give you some home-made plum jam to rub in that hair of yours.

If it don't cure your dandruff, you'll be bald within the month, and then you'll not need to worry no more, will you?

And if you're on the look-out for a spare bit of fluff, just you have a word with old Winston here and he'll fix you up in next to no time. If you're not averse to buck teeth and bandy legs, I knows an old boiler what would be only too willing to oblige.

Now then I'll bid you good day and continue my tour of inspection.

He walks out, followed by a distraught Nancy

Now this'll be the...

Nancy You can't go in there.

That's Rosie's studio.

No-one goes in Rosie's studio when she's working.

He steps inside

Oh, my Lord.

Rosie is working at a drawing board

Winston (*clacking his tongue with appreciation*) Well now, and what
feast of delection and delight has we got here, I asks myself.
Nancy (*hurriedly*) Rosie.
Rosie, this is the workman.
Rosie Hallo.
I'm Rosie.
Winston And I'm Winston.
Pleased to make your acquaintance. That I am.
Nice hooter you got there.
Rosie Pardon?
Winston Your hooter. Your nose look.
Very tasty. Do wonders for a man with a long tongue, that.
You a drawer by any chance.
You draw pictures?
Rosie (*amused*) No.
I make designs.
Winston So do I, missus.
I've made designs on every woman in this village look.
That I have without a doubt. And I got the bites on my ankles to prove
it. (*He laughs warmly*)

Rosie laughs too

Nancy Rosie! You're laughing!
You're laughing with a stranger. You never laugh with strangers.
You never laugh with us. You never ever laugh.
Winston Well, she's laughing now, missus.
And that's because she's with old Winston and in his company look.
Bits of fluff can't resist old Winston.
It's his blandishments, see.
You likes my blandishments, don't you, Rosie?
Bit of all right, ain't they?
Rosie (*surprised at herself*) Yes.
Yes, I suppose they are.

Winston Course they is.

(*To Nancy. Briskly*) Well then, missus, the electrics are up the spout here as well.

Same as in all the house.

Tell you what I'll do.

What I'll do is this—I'll completely re-wire from top to bottom for eight hundred and seventy-four pounds inclusive of Vee Ay Tee and VAT cash in hand.

Nancy How much?

Winston Well, you can take it or leave it, missus.

I'm not hiding nothing from you.

He'll be a messy job.

Same as when I does your roof.

Nancy I don't need the roof doing.

Winston Well then, on your head be it, missus.

This house, he's a danger to life and limb.

I'm surprised the council don't make you wear hard hats when you goes to the bogs.

Nancy How do you know so much about this house, Winston?

Winston Oh, everyone knows this house look.

Everyone in the village.

Old Wilson Rappaport, he had everyone back here sooner or later.

He used to have these parties down by his swimming pool.

Oh yes, everyone in the village came.

They'd get tanked up after a sesh at the pub and they'd stagger down here and they'd be jumping in the pool fully clothed and some of them, most noticeably the bints, they didn't have no clothes on at all.

Oh, he was a character old Wilson Rappaport.

He used to run the village fête, you know.

Rosie So we've been told.

Nancy Umpteen times.

Many, many times.

Winston So you would, missus.

That's because you'll be expected to run the fête now.

Rosie What?

Winston Well, I reckons it's a bit of a tradition in the village look.

Them what lives in this house has to organise the village fête.

Nancy Not any more, Winston.

Not any more.

We refuse categorically to have anything to do with the village fête.
And that is our final word on the subject.

Black-out

Lights up as Father wanders on, puffing at his pipe

Hammering and banging in the background

Father Hallo, house.
How are you getting on with all this hammering and banging.
It's that curious little wallah with the dirty wellies and the tattoos who's doing it.
Fearfully interesting tattoos he's got. One above each nipple.
Gin and Tonic.
Or is it Brandy and Soda? (*He sits down and examines his pipe*)
You know, house, I quite like you.
So does my pipe.
He draws well, you see.
Some houses I've lived in have been positively lethal to pipes.
Never drawn well. Never been able to get a suck at them.
They just smouldered and sulked and slucked.
A good pipe and a good house.
They go together like Gin and Tonic and Brandy and Soda and...
Mild and Bitter.
That's it. That's what he's got tattooed above his nipples.
Mild and Bitter.
Fearfully amusing, don't you think?

Lights down on him

Lights up on William typing away furiously in his study. The banging and hammering grow louder

Eventually, with a rumbling roar, Winston stumbles in, bearing a large sledgehammer

Winston Hallo, William.
Not disturbing you, am I?

William (*very painfully*) No, you're not disturbing me, Winston.
I'm only trying to write the penultimate chapter of my book.
Nothing important.

Winston Well, that's all right then.
Honest to God, William, I don't know how you writers manage to
write with all this noise and disturbance going on.
Can you write when people are talking to you?

William With great difficulty, Winston.
With enormous difficulty.

Winston Well, that's just like me look.
When I'm knocking a wall down or drilling a hole or attending to one
of my bits of fluff, I can work and talk all at the same time.
But when it comes to the important things like going down to the pub
for a sesh and a game of darts, I'm damned if I can talk and work at
the same time.
I expect that's just like you, is it, William?

William Well, sort of. Yes.

Winston What do you write books about then?
Mucky things?

William I beg your pardon?

Winston You knows, William.
Do you write them smutty things about Hollywood in the guise of a
lady novelist with wrinkled bristols?

William No.
No, as a matter of fact, Winston, I write books about railways.

Winston Oh, well you can get up to some rare old smutty goings-on on
railways, can't you?
I remember last time I went across to Yeovil the day after the village
fête.
I went with Betty Hayballs.
Cor! You know Betty Hayballs, do you, William?

William No, I can't say I do.

Winston You not met Betty Hayballs yet?
Well, you get a nice surprise coming to you and that's a fact.
She's what I call nice and juicy and ripe, if you follows my meaning
as regards her endowments.
She's my first cousin, too.
Well, there we are together in this empty compartment look, going
across to Yeovil and...

William That used to be on the Somerset and Dorset Line.
Winston What?
William Yeovil.
> It used to be on the Somerset and Dorset Line.
> They called it the Somerset and Dorset Committee.
> I'm writing a book about it.

Winston A serious book?
William Yes.
Winston You're writing a serious book about railways?
William Yes.
> That's how I earn my living.

Winston And they ain't smutty?
William Oh no.
Winston Well, that explains a lot, William.
> That certainly do explain a lot without a shadow of a doubt.

He wanders off thoughtfully

William resumes his typewriting. The hammering and banging starts off

Fade to Black-out

Nancy enters

Nancy (*to the audience*) The banging and hammering and drilling went
> on for days and days.
> And William did not once complain.
> How strange.
> How very curious.
> And Rosie didn't complain either.
> No paddies from her. No tantrums.
> She just smiled. And she looked radiant.
> Meanwhile, Father established himself in his shed and he whistled
> to himself and grinned at his pipe.
> Not a word of complaint.
> How strange. How curious.
> Not a murmur from his legs or his sinuses.
> Of course he'd secured his supplies of gin from Stanley.
> We weren't supposed to know he was a secret drinker.

But we did.

Every house we moved from we'd find this great cache of empty gin bottles and Father would say "Goodness me, I wonder how they got there?"

Yes.

Oh yes, things couldn't be all that strange if Father were still tippling at his gin.

Fade up the Lights on Father in the garden

Father Nancy, Nancy!

Nancy Yes, Father? Where are you?

Father Over here. In the garden.

Nancy Ah, there you are.

What do you want, Father?

Have you run out of Smarties? Have you burnt a hole in your *Daily Telegraph* again?

Father No.

I was just wanting to ask you something.

Nancy What?

Father It's about the swimming pool at the bottom of the garden there. Are we going to keep it?

Nancy I don't know.

Why do you ask?

Father Well, you know that wallah who's knocking holes in the walls and using up all the toilet paper?

Nancy Winston.

Father That's him—Winston.

Fearfully amusing tattoos he's got above his nipples.

Rum and Pep.

Nancy Mild and Bitter, Father.

And what about him?

Father Well, he was telling me yesterday that this pond is very probably a breeding place for sleeping sickness and beri beri.

Indeed, he's quite convinced that it was responsible for an outbreak of terminal squitters in Yeovil last year.

Nancy Really, Father?

Father Yes.

Reminds me very much of a stagnant pond I once knew when I lived in India with your mother when she was alive.

We were staying in this rest house.

Up in the hills.

Or was it the plains?

I don' t remember.

But there was a stagnant pond there and this frightfully pleasant old Indian cove came up to me and doffed his panama and said:

"No goee into pondee, Sahib."

And I said "No?"

"And why not, old chap?"

And he said "Very bad diseases there, Sahib."

And I said:

"Oh?"

"Malaria?"

And he said:

"Yes."

Very interesting conversation that was, Nancy.

Didn't speak to him again.

Pity.

I rather regretted that.

I felt that we had a certain something between us.

Don't you think so?

Nancy (*gently*) Yes, Father. Of course I do.

Another helicopter roars overhead

Father I say, another helicopter.

This really is a very very pleasant spot you've dragged us to, Nancy.

Fearfully pleasant. Well done.

Right then, toodle pip, old boy.

I'm off to my shed.

Important business to attend to.

He shuffles off

Nancy (*to the audience*) I feel cold.

I'm shivering.

Why am I shivering?

(*She pauses. Then fearfully*) Someone's watching me.

(*She turns rapidly*) Go away. Go away. Stop watching me. Stop looking at me.

(*She pauses*) I can feel this draught all over me, yet there's no breeze.
Look at that spider's web on the standard rose.
It's swaying backwards and forwards.
Backwards and forwards, yet there's no wind.
Stop watching me. Stop it, stop it.
Stop watching me.

Black-out

Lights up on the drawing room

Father is reading. Rosie is sewing. Nancy is punching the cushions and generally fussing

William enters

William I've finished my book.
    It's my best yet.
Rosie I'm very pleased for you, William.
    I'm thrilled.
Nancy There's no need to be sarcastic, Rosie.
Rosie I'm not being sarcastic.
    I mean it.
    It's the same with me.
    I'm producing the best designs I've ever done in my life.
William I think it must be the house.
    It is. It's the house.
    I really like it.
Nancy What?
    You like the house?
William Yes.
    It's got a certain ambience about it which makes me feel comfortable
    and at ease.
Rosie And creative.
William That's it—creative.
Father And happy, too.
Nancy What?
Father Happy, Nancy.
    I think we're all most fearfully happy, don't you?

Nancy Happy?

> You happy?
>
> I'm not listening to this nonsense a moment longer.
>
> I'm going to the kitchen to make cocoa for Father.

She exits into the kitchen

> Happy?
>
> At ease with the world?
>
> What's come over them?
>
> They've never ever been happy and contented and at ease with the world.
>
> Never never wherever we've lived.
>
> They've always quarrelled and griped and complained and...
>
> If they're happy, where do I fit in?
>
> What role do I have to play in their lives?
>
> What role do I have to play in my own life?

Ring on the front door

> I'll answer it. I'll go.
>
> You get on with being happy.

She goes to the front door and opens it

> *Standing there are Stanley, Janet and Mrs Godwin. Mrs Godwin is an elegant woman, tall and deeply seductive. She is the same age as William*

> Oh, Stanley. Janet.

Stanley Hallo.

> Nice to meet you again.
>
> And I'm sure Janet feels the same way, too.

Janet Oh yes.

> It's really nice to see you.
>
> And William and Stanley have become such good friends, haven't you, Stanley?

Stanley I should say we have.

> And so have your father and I.

I run him these small messages from time to time.

Fascinating chap, your father. He's got an endless fund of fascinating stories about India, you know.

Nancy Yes, Stanley, I am aware of that.

Stanley Good, good.

I wonder if I could introduce you to Mrs Godwin?

She's the lady who's standing on my left.

The opposite side to Janet.

Nancy How do you, Mrs Godwin.

My name's Nancy Empson.

Mrs Godwin How do you do?

I've heard such a lot about your brother and sister and father from Stanley here.

I'm longing to meet them.

Nancy Then may I invite you inside to meet them and take a drink with us?

Mrs Godwin How very kind.

Nancy Do come in.

And I apologise for Father well in advance.

She ushers them into the drawing room

Father, Rosie, William—we've got a visitor.

May I introduce Mrs Godwin. Stanley and Janet you already know.

Stanley in particular, eh, Father?

They shake hands and murmur greetings. Mrs Godwin lingers over William

Mrs Godwin Well, William, it's a great pleasure to meet you at long last.

Stanley's told me such a lot about you.

He lent me one of your books.

William (*deeply nervous of her sexuality*) Oh yes?

Which one?

Mrs Godwin I can't quite remember.

I think it was about railways.

Stanley Yes, well, yes, I took the liberty of inviting Mrs Godwin over here because she's what I call quite a big cheese as regards the village fête.

Nancy The village fête!

Not that again?

Janet Don't you like village fêtes?

Nancy No, we do not, do we, Rosie?

Rosie Oh, I don't know, Nancy.

I think they could be quite fun, if we let ourselves go.

Nancy What?

What's that you say?

Let ourselves go? We never let ourselves go.

Our family's noted for never letting ourselves go.

Mrs Godwin Well, we can easily change that.

You must come to one of my parties.

Everyone lets themselves go at my parties.

They're quite well-known for it in the village, aren't they, Stanley?

Stanley Yes.

Yes, they are, although I hasten to add that Janet and I do not partake of them very frequently, do we, Janet?

Janet No.

We're more of the stay-at-home type.

Mrs Godwin I know you are, Janet.

But perhaps William or Rosie or even Nancy might let themselves be tempted to one of our parties.

Rosie That would be nice.

Thank you.

Mrs Godwin I'm sure you'd enjoy them.

They're quite entertaining.

Quite novel really.

Father I like novel parties.

I once went to a frightfully novel party.

In India.

With your mother when she was alive.

It was in Goa.

Stanley Goa, eh?

Isn't that in India?

Father Yes.

The little black buggers who live there are Roman Catholics, you know.

It's an odd thing that.

You don't expect to find Roman Catholics in India, do you?

Muslims, yes. Hindus, Buddhists, Parsees, cricketers.

Oh yes, India's produced the most wonderful crop of cricketers in its time.

Engineer, Merchant, Contractor.

Curious. Curious the way their surnames are the names of trades and professions.

Though I don't ever recall an Indian Test cricketers called Furniture Remover.

I once saw the Indians play at Sevenoaks.

Or was it Eastbourne?

William Maidstone.

Father I beg your pardon, William?

William You saw them play at Maidstone, Father.

The Nawab of Pataudi scored seven.

Father Did he, by Jove?

How lovely for him.

(*He pauses*) Where was I?

Nancy Goa, Father.

You were in Goa.

Father Yes, yes, so I was.

Well, there we were in Goa, your mother and I and this chappie who made hat stands out of balsa wood.

Don't ask me why.

I suppose some people do and some people don't.

Anyway, there we were and...

He scored eleven.

Nancy Who, Father?

Father The Nawab of Pataudi.

He had the most exquisite range of strokes on the off side.

I wonder if he liked curry.

Nancy Father!

Father Yes, well, there we were in Goa on Ascension Day.

Or was it Shrove Tuesday?

It doesn't matter, I suppose.

Anyway, at this party they——

Nancy I hate parties.

I hate them. I hate them.

And I hate village fêtes, too.

Black-out

Hammering and typewriting. Hammering stops

Lights up to reveal William at work on another book

Winston enters

Winston I hear tell that Mrs Godwin visited you last night, William.
William (*testily stopping work*) What?
Winston That Mrs Godwin come round visiting.
    You knows—the good-looker with the big tits.
William I don't think I noticed them.
Winston What?
    You didn't notice them?
    Everyone else has look.
    Her berdongers are quite a feature of village life, William.
    Cor, I could tell you a thing or two about Mrs Godwin.
    She's the organiser in chief of all the village wife-swapping, she is.
William Wife-swapping?
Winston That's it—wife-swapping.
    It's rampant in the country, is wife-swapping.
    Not among my class, of course.
    But among you lot at this end of the village it's endemic look.
    And them mucky videos what you plays on the telly with a bag of
    crisps and your flies undone.
William What?
Winston There's no need to look so surprised, William.
    This is the country you're living in.
    It ain't the city.
    Last year ... oooh, last year within a radius of thirty odd miles of here
    we had two cases of murder, twenty-seven indecent exposures and
    God knows how many outbreaks of arson.
    It's quite a speciality in these parts, is arson.
    You'll love it once you gets used to it.
William Will I?
Winston Course you will.
    Specially when that Mrs Godwin gets her hands on you.
William What?
Winston That's why she come round, William, my old wingsy bash.
    To lay claim on you.
William What?
Winston Well, she had old Wilson Rappaport.
    So now he's snuffed it, she's going to have you.
    You comes with the house.
William I come with the house?

Winston Yes.

She was always round here, that Mrs Godwin.

Her and old Wilson Rappaport? Talk about cavorting? The bleeding Decameron, wasn't in it look.

Cor, I could tell you some tales about what they got up to what would make your hair stand on end.

And talking about that, you knows your sister?

William Which one?

Winston That Rosie.

William What about her?

Winston Is she courting?

William Pardon?

Winston Has she got a blokey?

A gentleman friend?

William No.

No, she hasn't.

Winston Right then, we'll soon see about that.

I will introduce myself to her tonight all dicky dolled up with clean socks and my underpants freshly done in Rinso and I shall ask her if she would like to accompany me on a sesh at the pub.

William But I thought you were married.

Winston Course I'm married.

What's that got to do with it?

My missus expects me to have my bits of fluff on the side.

It's part and parcel of being faithfully married to a woman what's as ugly as sin and never read a single word of the collected works of Jean Jacques Rousseau, the well-known philosopher.

William But Rosie isn't like that, Winston.

She wouldn't dream of going out with a married man.

Winston I wouldn't be too sure of that, William.

This is the country. You got to settle in our ways, ain't you?

And I believes that Rosie already has.

William Do you?

Winston Course I does.

You wait till I comes round tonight, and you'll see.

You wait and see what happens when old Winston comes to pay his court.

Fade out

Fade up the Lights back to the drawing room

Rosie is sketching. Father is smoking his pipe

Father It's evening.
      I like the evening. Rosie.
Rosie So do I.
      It's so peaceful. So contented.
Father Yes.
      Like the evening of my life now.
Rosie Are you really peaceful and contented, Father?
Father Oh yes.
      I like it here, Rosie.
Rosie So do I.
      I thought I was going to hate it.
      But now? Now I love it. I adore it.
      Why?
Father It's the house, Rosie.
      It's weaved its spell around us.
      It's beguiled us and enchanted us.
      Lovely, lovely house.
      A chap would be totally content to die in a house like this.
Rosie You're not going to die, Father.
      You're still in your prime.
      You're still young at heart.
Father I used to like being young.
Rosie Did you, Father?
Father Yes.
      Well, I was damned good at it, you see.
      I played my part at being young. No shirking. No backsliding.
      I had desires in the bath.
      I was a keen rambler.
      I liked making dams in mountain streams.
      I liked the smell of shaving soap.
      I liked slim ankles.
      Gold bangles round slim dusky ankles and olive skin and lips pouting
      with promise.
      Yes, those were the days, old boy.
      My God, I'd give anything to have spots and boils on the back of my
      neck again.

Front doorbell rings. They do not move. It rings again

Nancy enters

Nancy That's right, don't move, don't put yourselves out.
Nancy will answer it, won't she?
Of course she will.
Good old Nancy.
What would we do without her?

She goes to the front door and opens it

Winston is standing there. He is immaculately dressed in pink shirt with yellow fox-head cravat and blue corduroy suit. His hair is slicked and combed back

Winston!
Winston, is it you?
Winston That's right, missus.
I'm all dicky dolled up and squirted under me armpits with foot powder.
Nancy What do you want?
Winston I just called on the off chance, missus.
Nancy On the off chance, Winston?
Winston That's right.
Old Winston called on the off chance that your sister, Rosie, might like to go out with me this evening in my car, my motor look.
Nancy Rosie?
Rosie go out with you?
Winston Yes.
I'll show her a bit of the countryside look.
Show her some nice places off the beaten track.
Take her to the pub at the back of the abattoir.
A young girl like her, well, it's not right she should be stuck in on her own with a load of old fuddy duddies like you lot, is it?
She wants taking out of herself.
Wants her mind stimulating and her body refurbished and titillated.
Nancy How dare you.
How dare you, you disgusting squalid little man with your tattoos and your boozer's belly and your dirty ears.

How dare you insinuate that Rosie is in need of your stimulation.
We are a refined family.

We are an educated family.

I've been to Florence and Switzerland before sweets were off the ration.

I've been to the National Theatre three times and I think Alan Ayckbourn's *The Caretaker* is the best thing he's ever written.

Winston Harold Pinter.

Nancy What?

Winston It was Harold Pinter what wrote *The Caretaker*.

Nancy All right, all right.

I don't suppose he cares who wrote it just as long as it's performed in public.

Winston Cor blimey, Charlie, you don't half look tasty when you got your rag out.

Nancy What?

Winston You looks really desirable, missus. You looks really bold and handsome and redolent and juicy and ripe.

You don't fancy coming out with me instead of Rosie, do you?

Nancy Go away.

Go away, you dreadful, appalling little man.

Winston Certainly, missus. As you wish.

(*He turns to go, then stops*) Oh, there's just one other thing, though.

Nancy What?

Winston I been thrown out of my house.

Nancy What?

Winston The missus have gone and turfed me out lock, stock and barrel.

Nancy What?

Winston The missus. My missus.

You knows her—the ugly old party with the blotches and the congenital knees.

Nancy What?

Winston I wish you wouldn't keep saying "What", Nancy.

It's perfectly simple look.

My missus have objected—took umbrage look—to my bits of fluff.

Nancy Your bits of fluff?

Winston Yes. The women I has on the side. My bits of fluff.

Everyone knows about old Winston's bits of fluff.

Nancy Now then, Winston, let's get this straight.

Your wife has thrown you out of the house because she objects to your infidelities, is that right?

Winston In a manner of speaking.

It's like Madame Bovary only in reverse look.

Nancy I don't understand, Winston.

Winston It's simple, Nancy.

My missus have at long last took the hump on account of my constant and never-ending gallivanting and have got herself a blokey.

Nancy A blokey?

Winston Yes.

Gilbert Spurfield from the ironmongers.

He moved in this dinner time with his stamp collection and his hover mower.

Nancy Well ... well, I don't quite know what to say, Winston.

I mean, have you thought what you're going to do?

Have you made any plans?

Winston Yes.

Nancy What?

Winston I'm going to move in here with you.

Nancy What?

Winston It's the best thing all round, Nancy.

Couldn't have worked out better look.

I comes to live with you, and you've got me constantly on hand, haven't you?

I'll do all your renovations and repairs in situ as we say in the trade. I'll wait on at table. I'll drive you round in my car, my motor look and explain to you in simple terms the life and times of the Venetian Empire, twelve-o-two to seventeen ninety-seven.

Nancy But ... but...

Winston Right then, Nancy.

My gear's in my car, my motor look.

I'll just go and fetch it and...

Nancy. Nancy, there's no need to look all worried and perplexed.

I had a word about it with your father and Rosie and William.

I squared it with them and they're delighted.

They're like pigs in shit look.

Nancy But ... but...

Winston (*moving very close to her*) I'll look after you, Nancy.

Leave it to old Winston, missus.

He'll cosset you and he'll pamper you and he'll give you all his love and all his tenderness.

And another thing.

Nancy What?

Winston I'll help you organise the village fête.

Nancy The village fête!

Oh my God, that bloody village fête!

CURTAIN

ACT II

Father is pottering slowly round the garden smoking his pipe

A dog is barking in the distance

Father That dog's been barking non-stop for the last two weeks.
It's Winston's dog.
He says it's barking because it misses him.
How pleasant to be missed.
I once had a dog who missed me in India.
Fearful brute he was.
He ate the steering wheel of our neighbour's Frazer Nash tourer.
Or was it a Wolsley Convertible?

Nancy (*calling*) Father, Father, where are you?

Father (*calling*) In the garden, old boy.

Nancy (*calling*) What are you doing?

Father (*to himself*) What am I doing?
If I knew the answer to that, my dear, I'd be a happy man.
So would everyone else in the world.
We'd be happy, content and live in total peace with each other.
With a bit of luck we could achieve the ultimate bliss—we could all
be the Nawab of Pataudi scoring seven runs on a sunlit afternoon in
Sevenoaks.
Or is it Maidstone?

Nancy (*calling*) Father, come inside.
You'll catch your death of cold.

Father (*calling*) Coming, old boy. Coming.
(*He begins to potter off, then pauses*) I once saw a woman with no
togs in Karachi. Magnificent sight.
She was the spitting image of Herbert Sutcliffe.

He enters the drawing room and joins Nancy, William, and Rosie

What-ho, chaps.

Rosie Hallo, Father.

We're just talking about Winston.

Nancy A real old mess, isn't it?

Rosie Well, you've only yourself to blame, Nancy.

You're the one who invited him to stay.

Nancy I did not invite Winston to stay, Rosie.

He invited himself.

He just barged past me with his cardboard boxes and his black plastic bin bags bursting at the seams and now... and now...

William And now he's keeping me awake all night snoring his head off and whistling through his teeth in the spare bedroom.

Father Well, bung him in the shed then.

William What?

Father Bang him in the shed at the bottom of the garden.

That's what we did with blighters like him in India.

The shed in the bottom of the garden in India was always full of them—little brown buggers all crouched up in their underpants and staring at their big toenails.

Nancy Father, please.

Oh crumbs, what a state to get ourselves in.

Rosie Well, there's only one thing for it.

William And what's that, Rosie?

Rosie We'll have to hold a family conference.

Father A family conference!

I say—how splendid.

I love family conferences. Fearfully interesting.

If I should fall asleep, there's no need to bother waking me up.

Rosie Right, Consider the family conference convened.

Now, the way I see the problem is this—Winston is now firmly established in this house.

So do we want things to stay that way or do we want to change them?

And if so, how do we go about doing it?

Do we reason with him?

Do we threaten him?

Father We could always shoot him.

Rosie What?

Father Or we could get one of those helicopter chappies to take him up in his machine and drop him out over the mushroom farm.

William He'd bounce.

Father What?

William He'd bounce right back into the helicopter with a great trium-
phant grin on his face, and then he'd try to sell the pilot the services
of his disgusting second cousin at Chippenhan Junction.

At special discount price, too.

Rosie Don't be so idiotic, the two of you.

Let's try and be sensible and cool and calm and collected for a
change, shall we?

Let's each of us in turn give our opinion about whether Winston
should stay or whether Winston should go.

Right then, Nancy. Over to you.

Nancy What?

What's that you say?

Rosie You've not been listening, have you?

You've not heard a word I've said.

Nancy I'm sorry, Rosie. How rude of me.

It's just that I'm... I'm ... all those memories.

It's so strange.

They've just come flooding back.

Rosie (*warmly*) What memories, Nancy?

Nancy Memories of our last house in London.

Father Ah yes, I remember that. Fearfully pleasant place.

It had those exquisite wrought iron balconies and a wonderful view
out over the harbour with the fishing smacks bobbing in the bay
and...

Rosie That was Scarborough, Father.

Scarborough. Or was it Morecambe.

God, he's got me going now. He's got...

(*Softly*) Go on, Nancy. Go on.

Nancy I was thinking about the house spider.

The day we moved out he disappeared.

I wonder if the new people have looked after him?

I wonder if he's happy.

Rosie I expect he is, Nancy.

Spiders don't look the miserable sort to me.

Nancy (*laughing gently*) Yes, Rosie, yes.

And then I got round to thinking about the day we moved in here and
the gas leak and the poor old boiler being condemned and looking so
wretched about it.

And we sat here in the cold on packing cases with night lights because all the fuses had blown.

And then Winston came round with his lovely smile and the nicotine stains on the palms of his hands.

And one day I looked out of my bedroom window, and there he was straddled across the roof of the stables ripping off the slates with his funny hammer and he was singing at the top of his voice, and he was wearing the most ghastly canary yellow socks all wrinkled at the ankles, and he looked so happy.

I'd never seen anyone look so happy.

I didn't know people could look so happy.

I'm a mature woman, and I didn't realize people could look happy without feeling guilty.

William Yes, Nancy, yes.

It's all very well going sentimental on us, but what we need now is the practical approach.

I detest Winston's socks just as much as you do.

But the manner in which he clads his feet is not the issue at stake.

What we've got to decide is our attitude towards his presence in the house.

Father Can I smell burning?

Nancy What?

Father I can smell burning.

Rosie It's you, Father.

There's a spark fallen from your pipe and set alight to your cardigan. Stay where you are, and I'll put you out.

She flaps at him to put him out

Father Jolly Dee.

Do you know, chaps, it amazes me that the boffins haven't considered inventing a fireproof cardigan for the use of inveterate pipe smokers.

William Will you please shut up and listen to me.

Father Certainly, old boy. Certainly.

You know, he's just like his mother, only he's not got a hairy chest and he doesn't play golf.

Rosie Father!

Father Sorry, William.

As you were. Carry on.

William Well, all I've got to say is that I think Winston's a good sort.
   He's been a real brick to us.
   He's helped us out of the most dreadful mess here in the house.
   He's helped us settle in and understand the ways of the country.
   I look on him as a friend.
   A close friend. He's taught me how to french kiss.
   But ... but...

Rosie But what?

William He can't stay here.

Rosie Why not?

William Because he's not our sort.

Rosie Why?

William Good grief, Rosie, it's obvious.

Rosie Not to me.

William Of course it is. You know perfectly well that he's uncouth and
   vulgar and ... and...

Rosie Common?

William Common. Exactly.
   Winston might be the salt of the earth.
   He might have a heart of gold.
   But deep down, basically, he is irredeemably common.
   He is not our sort.

Rosie What a disgustingly snobbish thing to say.

William Is it really?

Rosie Yes, it is.

William No it isn't.

Nancy Will you two stop quarrelling.
   Why can't we do anything together without quarrelling, without
   falling out and shouting and screaming at each other?
   Why?
   Why are we always so angry with each other?
   Why do we suspect happiness so much?
   Why do we hate it and fear it?
   Why can't we be like Winston—simple, direct, totally gluttonous for
   happiness?
   Winston!
   Winston, so full of love and mischief.
   Winston, so full of love and...

He's got to go.

Rosie What?

Nancy It's quite out of the question for him to stay here.

Rosie Why?

Nancy Because ... because ... well, because he doesn't fit in.

William Exactly, Nancy. Precisely.

Nancy He doesn't belong here.

He'd dirty. He's smelly. His manners are appalling. He's rude.
He's disrespectful. He's...

*Winston enters. He is wearing an alpaca jacket and pin-striped trousers
and his hair is sleeked back*

Winston Ladies and gentlemen, supper is served.

That he is without a doubt.

(*He pushes in a trolley groaning with food*) Just a little something
what I knocked up look.

Right then, I'll tell you what everything is, just so's you'll know what
you're supposed to be eating.

If you'd like to wake up your dad, Rosie, I shall now commence and
begin.

Right then, you have a choice of starters.

Pickled salmon, *canapés à la crème* or a nice fricassee of eggs.

Now then, for your joint you've got roast pork with pistachio nuts or
you might like to try the chicken liver with grapes provided you've
got a strong stomach and don't mind the pips.

Now then for your vegetables you got asparagus with new pota-
toes—or spuds as we calls them in the trade—and you got savoury
cucumber and a chilled haricot bean salad.

For dessert you has a choice of gooseberry flan or choice French
cheeses freshly garnered from the back end of a container lorry at
Poole Harbour this very morning.

Well, don't sit there looking all gormless.

Get stuck in and enjoy yourselves.

And I don't mind if you has a good fart when you've finished look.

Nancy Winston, this is incredible. It's amazing. It's fantastic.

Winston All right, all right.

No need to make a bleeding meal of it.

Oh, and before I goes there' s something else what I has to impart.

Rosie What's that, Winston?

Winston I have completed all the household chores.

I've washed and ironed all the bedding, I've got you a brand new freezer from unnamed sources, I've put a new ribbon in William's typewriter and as for you two ladies, I've put your knickers to soak in fabric softener in a bucket in the utility room.

I wish you *bon appétit* and would ask you during the course of the meal to refrain from sticking your gilberts on the corners of the tablecloth.

Good night.

He exits

William I don't believe this.

I just don't believe it.

Father I do.

I say. Asparagus. Whacko.

This reminds me of a feast I once had in Rangoon when...

Nancy Father.

Father Yes, old boy?

Nancy Shut up and eat.

Father Certainly, old boy. Ready, steady, Go.

Fade out the Lights as they all tuck in with gusto and delight

Fade up the Lights back on the garden

   Winston is sitting on the wall

Rosie enters from the drawing room

Rosie I'm so full. I'm bursting. I'm... (*She spots Winston*) Winston.

Winston Hayballs, that was the most delicious meal I have had for years and years and years.

It was gorgeous.

Winston Thank you, Rosie.

And I hope you won't be kept up with it all night.

Rosie I won't, Winston. It was lovely.

She kisses him on his forehead

Winston That was nice.

Rosie Was it?

Winston Yes. It felt as though you really meant it.

Rosie I did.

Winston Why?

Rosie Because they've decided they want you to stay and that makes me happy.

Winston Good.

Do you want to stick your tongue in my ear then?

Rosie No. (*She laughs*)

Winston laughs

Winston You not got a regular blokey then, Rosie?

Rosie No.

Winston Have you ever had a regular blokey?

Rosie Oh yes.

Winston Was he a nice blokey?

Rosie I thought so.

Winston What did he do then, this blokey of yours?

Rosie He was a pilot in the RAF.

Winston Oh.

He flew aeroplanes, did he?

Rosie Yes.

He crashed and got killed.

Winston Happens to the best of them, Rosie.

Them boys, they goes up in them planes and half the time they don't know what's what, do they?

Rosie No, they don't.

Winston I knows what's what, though. Rosie.

Rosie Do you, Winston? What do you know?

Winston I knows you're a very beautiful young woman, Rosie.

(*He begins to edge towards her*) I knows you makes the sap rise in my loins.

I knows you...

Rosie Have you got any children, Winston?

Winston (*backing away sharply*) What?

Rosie Have you got any children?

Winston Yes. Eight.

Rosie Eight?

Winston That's right.

And another on the way.

All as ugly as sin, every one of them.

Takes after their mother see.

Rosie Have you lived here all your life?

Winston Oh yes. Without a doubt I have, Rosie.

Rosie Do you like it here?

Winston Well, I don't know nothing different, do I?

Rosie No.

You're very lucky really.

Winston Course I am.

Listen to me, Rosie, every day I gets up at five in the morning.

And in the summer and in the spring I goes down to the bottom of my garden and there's a wood there.

A little wood look.

And I goes deep inside him and I hears the birds singing.

Chiff chaffs, willow warblers, nightjars churring away.

And I sits down with my back against this old beech tree and I listens to them.

And I thinks to myself:

You're dead lucky, you little buggers.

If you was any bigger I'd shoot you with my shotgun quick as look at you and have you in my stock pot.

Rosie (*laughing*) Winston!

Winston And when I done that, Rosie, I goes back inside the house and I has my breakfast.

A slice of dripping toast and a glass of port.

Rosie A glass of port for breakfast?

Winston Oh yes, without a doubt, Rosie.

A slice of dripping toast and a glass of port for breakfast—do you all the good in the world.

You wants to try it.

Build you up it will.

Put a bit of flesh on you.

A bit more flesh on you up top, my dear, and you'd be the apple of old Winston's eye.

Rosie Well, I might just try it, Winston.

Winston Course you should.

All my bits of fluff, they all has a wallop at the old dripping toast and port.

Well, they wants to keep well in with old Winston, don't they?

Rosie I suppose they do, Winston.

You're quite a regular guy after all.

Winston Oh that I am without a shadow of a doubt.

Can I tell you something, Rosie?

Something personal.

Rosie Yes.

What is it?

Winston You ain't got no stench pipe.

Rosie What?

Winston You ain't got no stench pipe.

At the back of your house.

Old Wilson Rappaport, he took it down.

Why, I do not know.

Tell you what, though, Rosie.

Rosie What?

Winston I'll put you one in.

Free and gratis.

Just for you, Rosie.

Free and gratis.

Rosie Thank you, Winston.

That's the best offer I've had in years.

Winston Yes, well, I always likes to look after my bits of fluff, don't I?

Tell you something else, Rosie.

Rosie What's that, Winston?

Winston Give us a kiss like what you done before and I'll get you a new gas boiler.

Rosie Free and gratis?

Winston Free and gratis, Rosie.

Without a doubt.

They kiss. Black-out

Next morning in the garden

Nancy (*to the audience*) What's going on?

What is going on?

Winston has just arrived with a new gas boiler.
And he's putting it in now.
And he's not going to charge us for it.
He said it was free and gratis.
And he smiled at me and winked.
And Rosie smiled, too.
What on earth is going on?
Smiling faces and laughter—I don't understand.

William enters with a great beam on his face

William, you're smiling.
William That's right, Nancy. (*He bends down and starts picking flowers*)
Nancy What on earth are you doing?
William Picking flowers.
Nancy What for?
William For my visitor.
Nancy Visitor?
You're having a visitor?
Who?
William Er … er … Mrs Godwin.
Nancy Mrs Godwin?
William Yes.
Why shouldn't I?
What's wrong with it?
What's…
(*He composes himself and says firmly*) I'm having a visitor, Nancy.
And I do not wish to be disturbed.

He exits purposefully

Nancy (*gazing after him totally bewildered*) What's happening?
What's happening to us all?

Fade out

Fade up the Lights back to the drawing room where William is with Mrs Godwin

William I hope you like the tea, Mrs Godwin.

Mrs Godwin It's lovely, William.

Clever old you.

William Oh, I didn't make it.

Winston made it.

He was wearing Nancy's pinnie when he cut the crusts off the sandwiches and...

Would you perhaps care for something a little stronger, Mrs Godwin?

Mrs Godwin Thank you, William, no.

Not at four in the afternoon.

Stronger things come later in the day, don't they, William?

William Yes.

Yes, I suppose they do, Mrs Godwin.

Mrs Godwin I'd much rather you called me Lucy, William.

William Certainly.

Only too happy to oblige, Lucy.

Mrs Godwin Are you well ahead with your preparations for the village fête, William?

William No. Not really.

Well, Winston's taking care of all that, you see.

I don't go in for things like that.

None of the family does.

We're very private people, you see.

Mrs Godwin But it's expected of you.

William Yes, I rather gathered that.

Mrs Godwin It's expected of the house.

Mr Rappaport virtually organised the whole village fête himself.

William Yes, but I'm not like Mr Rappaport.

Mrs Godwin No?

William No.

Mrs Godwin In what way are you different from Wilson... Mr Rappaport?

William I ... I like to keep myself to myself.

I like my own company.

Well, present company excepted, of course.

Mrs Godwin Are you a single man, William?

William Yes.

I always have been.

All my life. From birth.

I always will be, I suppose.

Mrs Godwin And why is that?

William I don't seem to have time for it.

I'm very busy with my books, you see.

Mrs Godwin Ah.

William What people don't realize is that it's not only the writing of the book which takes up your time, it's the research.

There's a great deal of research to be done.

Before I start writing a book I always do my research in loco and... (*He laughs*)

In loco?

That's not a bad joke for someone who writes books about railways, is it?

Mrs Godwin It's very good.

(*She pauses*) Do you like village life, William?

William Yes.

I didn't at first, though.

Mrs Godwin No?

William No.

You see I didn't want to come here.

And neither did Rosie if the truth be known.

We came because of Father.

His chest.

We always seem to be moving because of Father.

We lived at the seaside and had to leave because of his sinus.

We lived in the North Country and had to leave because of his legs.

Mrs Godwin His legs?

William It was the hills, you see.

He couldn't get up them.

Which was rather a pity because we lived on top of a hill.

If we'd lived at the bottom, it might have been different.

Mrs Godwin And what about Nancy?

William Nancy?

Mrs Godwin Nancy.

How does she fit in?

Does she like moving house?

William Oh no, she...

It's strange you should say that.

Mrs Godwin Why?

William Well, until we moved here I always thought she hated moving as much as Rosie and I did. And then...

Well, I looked at her the other day and it suddenly dawned on me:

She liked moving.
Deep down she really liked it.
Mrs Godwin Why did you think that, William?
William I don't know.
It was just a feeling I had that she likes to keep us on our toes.
Keep us from settling in anywhere.
Keep us from being happy.
Because when we're not happy, she takes charge, you see.
She's the boss.
She has a role to play.
And now we're happy and contented, she's not wanted.
She's not needed.
She's...
What a dreadful thing to say.
I'm sorry. It's very disloyal of me.
And yet... And yet.

Pause

Mrs Godwin I wonder if you'd like to come to one of my parties, William.
William Pardon?
Mrs Godwin I'm giving a party tonight.
William Tonight?
Mrs Godwin Yes.
An impromptu party.
William Will Stanley and Janet be there?
Mrs Godwin No.
William Oh.
Will there be anyone I know at the party?
Mrs Godwin Yes.
William Who?
Mrs Godwin I'll be there.
Just me.
William Just you?
Just you on your own?
Mrs Godwin Yes. Just me. On my own.
Do come round, William. Eight o'clock would be lovely.
You can explain all the finer points about your books.
Finer points?
That's a good joke about books on railways, isn't it?

Fade out

Fade up the Lights on Nancy in the garden

Nancy (*to the audience*) I'm at a loss.
I am. I'm completely at a loss.
Everything's topsy-turvy.
William had his visitor this afternoon and he was smirking all over his face.
And now he's gone out dressed in his white linen suit and his spotted handkerchief and he's grinning all over his face.
And Rosie's grinning, too.
And...

Winston appears, scurrying towards the shed

Winston.
Winston Yes, Nancy?
Nancy Why are you grinning all over your face?
Winston Cos I'd look daft grinning all over my backside, wouldn't I?
Nancy Winston, how dare you use such language.
I will not...
Winston Sorry, Nancy.
I got no time to be given a bollocking at the moment.
I'm off to see your father in his shed.
Urgent business, see. Yes, urgent business.

He exits

Nancy Urgent business?
Urgent business with Father?
The whole world's going mad.

Cross-fade to Father smoking in his shed

Winston knocks on the door

Father Come in. It's only me.

Winston enters

Winston How do then? What do you reckon? Not a lot.

Father Ah, Winston, splendid to see you, old boy.

Winston (*sniffing hard*) Have you been drinking secret again?

Father Good Lord, no, no.

Gave that up days ago.

I feel like a new man.

My socks are dry. There's no slucking in the bottom of my pipe.

I haven't burned a single hole in the front of my cardigan.

What on earth am I going to do with my life now?

Winston Well, you could always get yourself a bit of fluff.

Father I beg your pardon?

Winston Get yourself a bit of fluff.

Bring her back to your shed.

Betty Hayballs—she's the one for you look.

She'd turn a few holes for you in the front of your cardigan.

Father No, no, I'm far too old for that, old boy.

It's my chest, you see. It's my sinuses. It's my...

And yet?

(*He chuckles*) Ah, happy memories. Happy memories.

Winston Tell me something.

Father What?.

Winston Has you ever been unfaithful in your life?

Father Yes.

Once.

With Mrs Ventris.

In India.

She was a half chat.

Winston Ah.

A touch of the old tar brush, eh?

Father Yes.

She was the wife of the local station master.

In India.

She was a very tall woman.

She had long legs and a slim body and a rather large backside.

She'd have made the most wonderful fast bowler, if only she'd been a man.

Winston That's the whole tragedy of the history of Test cricket, ain't it?

Father Ah, Mrs Ventris!

I used to go to the station every morning without fail.

I used to like to see the Night Mail to Madras flash by.

Or was it the Bombay Mail?

I suppose that's where William's got it from.

Winston Watching trains?

Father No, no, having a penchant for tall slim ladies with long legs and expressive chests.

Winston Oh, that Mrs Godwin, eh?

Father No, no, Mrs Ventris, old boy.

She was the one who lived in India.

(*He chuckles*) Yes, I used to go to the station every morning and sit on the bench.

And one morning Mrs Ventris brought me a pot of tea and a sandwich.

And I suddenly realized what superb ears she'd got.

They were very large and pendulous.

Winston Yes, I knows all about ears like that.

Get your tongue in them something chronic, can't you?

Father What?

(*He pauses, then smiles softly*) Anyway, she brought me this pot of tea and the sandwich and something stirred in me.

I hadn't felt so roused since ... since I saw Ranji score a ton at Canterbury.

And she smiled at me and she said:

"Mr Ventris is away on business."

And she beckoned me.

And I followed her through the booking hall and into their private quarters.

It smelled of patchouli.

And there was a parakeet on a stand and an old lady in a wicker armchair smoking a cheroot.

She took me into the bedroom.

There was an alpaca jacket hanging from a hook at the bottom of the door.

It looked so forlorn, so cheated, so humiliated. (*He pauses*) Where was I?

Winston In the bedroom.

With this half caste bint.

Father Ah. Yes.

Yes, she took off her togs.

And so did I.

We stood there naked.

It was like being in the changing room before the first game of rugger
I ever played at prep school.

Yes. Yes.

And then the Night Mail roared through the station.

The buildings shook and rumbled.

And I was unfaithful.

I was unfaithful twice.

On the trot.

Fade out

Fade up the Lights. It is next morning

*Nancy is in the garden. Father is sitting in a deck chair, smoking. Rosie
is at an easel sketching*

Nancy (*to the audience*) What were they talking about in the shed last
night?

What on earth was their urgent business?

I left them to it.

I went to bed early.

And I dreamed.

I dreamed about mother.

How curious.

I hadn't thought of her for years and years.

Mother with her pinched little face and her dumpy golfer's legs.

And she was laughing.

And Father was there, too, and he was laughing.

And quite suddenly Winston appeared.

And he was wearing an alpaca jacket and smoking a cheroot, and he
had a green parakeet on his shoulder, and he was laughing, too.

Everyone was laughing.

Everyone.

Why?

Why is everyone laughing?

*William enters cackling with self-satisfied mirth. He's twirling and
swirling*

William I like it here.

I love it here.

Nancy William, for heaven's sake, what's the matter with you?

Dancing round like that and you're still wearing your pyjama jacket.

William I don't care.

I'm happy, Nancy.

Happy, happy.

I've never been so happy in the whole of my life.

It's wonderful here.

Absolutely wonderful.

Father Yes.

Yes, I think it's wonderful, too.

Nancy You, Father?

Father Certainly, old boy.

Sleeping fearfully well since we moved here.

Never slept better.

Didn't sleep too well last night, mind you.

You came home very late, William.

You were whistling as you went upstairs.

Nancy Were you?

I didn't hear you come back.

It must have been very late, William.

Where had you been?

William Er ... er ... to see Mrs Godwin.

Nancy Mrs Godwin!

What were you doing there?

William Er ... er ... talking about arrangements for the village fête.

Nancy The village fête?

William Yes.

It's expected of us, Nancy.

And there's not long to go now, you know.

Nancy But we're not having anything to do with the village fête.

We decided that ages ago.

Rosie Oh, I don't think we decided it absolutely, did we, Nancy?

Nancy What?

Rosie I think we should make the effort.

As a matter of fact, I've volunteered to help Winston on the hoop-la stall.

Nancy The hoop-la stall?

You?

Making a fool of yourself like that?

Rosie Why not?

William Exactly. Why not?

I've sort of volunteered to help Mrs Godwin actually.

Nancy Have you?

William Yes.

On the bring-and-buy stall.

I thought I'd donate a couple of my books.

And Mrs Godwin suggested I stay there and volunteer to autograph them.

It should be fun.

I'll be helping out, you see.

Father Yes, I think I might potter down there, too.

Could always make myself useful, if I don't get in the way.

I remember going to a bazaar once.

In India.

With your mother when she was still alive.

It was in Goa and there was a chap making hat stands out of balsa wood and...

Nancy Yes, Father, we've heard that story before.

Many times.

Times without number.

Rosie There's no need to snap at Father like that.

Nancy I'm not snapping.

Rosie Yes, you are.

I used to be an expert on snapping.

And I know when people are snapping.

Nancy Used to be? Used to be?

Oh dear.

Oh dear, oh dear.

William Are you all right, Nancy?

Nancy I don't know.

I feel a little strange.

I think I'm all right.

But I'm not quite sure.

I think I'll sit down for a while in my sewing room.

The Lights follow her into her sewing room. She sits down

I feel so lonely.

I feel so alone.

Why didn't I marry Geoffrey when I had the chance?

Why did he never propose to me?

He could have done.

I wouldn't have bitten his head off.

I only shouted at him when he forgot his table manners or fiddled with his wrist watch or...

Someone's watching me.

I can feel it.

I'm being watched.

And I'm being laughed at.

Two people are laughing at me.

A man and a woman.

I'm going to scream.

I can't stand it. I'm going to scream. (*She opens her mouth to scream*)

Winston enters

Winston Not disturbing you, am I, missus?

Nancy Winston!

Oh, Winston, I've just had the most horrible...

(*She composes herself*) What do you want?

Winston It's about your skirting board, missus.

He'll have to come up.

You see, if I'm to put a new rad in here, I've got to rip up your skirting board to get at the pipes look.

Nancy I didn't say anything about doing the rads.

Winston Oh yes, you did, missus.

It was all included in the new revised estimate what I give you the other day.

Put new rads in and make good.

Nancy I see.

I must have got it wrong.

Winston Not to worry.

It's no crime getting things wrong.

It's...

You're looking a bit pale, missus, if you don't mind me saying so.

Is this country air not agreeing with you?

Nancy Yes.

    Yes, it's agreeing with me.

    I suppose.

    Although on the other hand I... I...

Winston You wants to let yourself go, my dear, if you don't mind me saying.

    You got to join in look.

    You lives in the country now, and you got to join its ways.

    You can't be private and keep yourself to yourself.

    Folks don't like it.

    Neither does the birds and the flowers and the old chalk streams.

    Look at me, Nancy.

    I joins in.

    But you know what I am basically, deep down by trade and by inclination?

Nancy No.

Winston I'm a philosopher.

Nancy A philosopher?

Winston Oh yes.

    I been to the public library and read all the books about it.

    I'm a great reader look.

    I read books by people you never heard of.

    Jean Jacques Rousseau.

    He's someone you never heard of.

Nancy As a matter of fact, Winston, I have heard of him.

Winston Well then, that just shows what a lot we got in common, doesn't it?

Nancy What?

Winston I been watching you, Nancy.

Nancy Watching me?

Winston Yes.

    You 'asn't seen me.

    You hasn't noticed.

    But I been watching you.

    And I been thinking.

Nancy What have you been thinking?

Winston (*laughing*) Ooh, that'd be telling, wouldn't it, Nancy?

    And blokes like me don't tell much to women.

    They does to their bits of fluff mind.

Nancy Have you got many bits of fluff, Winston?
Winston Course I has.

That's why I don't practise being a philosopher.
Nancy I don't follow.
Winston It's simple, Nancy.

There's no money to be earned round here being a philosopher.

If you wants to earn money round here you got to chop down trees and shoot deers and rustle sheep and nick lead off the cathedral roof. That's the way to earn money.

And you got to have money if you wants to buy presents for your bits of fluff, ain't you?
Nancy I suppose you do.

And what sort of presents do you buy for your bits of fluff, Winston?
Winston Oh this and that.

A stench pipe here.

A new gas boiler there.

You're not wanting anything for the house by the way, are you, Nancy?

Black-out

Laughter

Lights up slowly to reveal Father smoking his pipe. He nods happily at William and Mrs Godwin who walk past hand in hand, smiling and laughing. He waves a greeting to Stanley and Janet who pass by gossiping happily. He smiles broadly at Rosie and Winston who, laughing and giggling, pass him and sit nearby on the wall

Father (*to the audience*) I like seeing the chaps happy.

Keeps up the *esprit de corps*, you know.

Fearfully good for morale, laughter.

My wife, when she was alive, never laughed. "I don't see the point of it", she used to say.

Those were her last words as she lay on her death bed.

"I don't see the point of it."

And I gazed down at her and she looked so angry, so dissatisfied, so disgruntled.

And then she popped off.

And I couldn't t help laughing.

Or was it the weeping I couldn't help?

He shuffles off, nodding to Winston and Rosie as he passes them

Rosie (*laughing*) I do love it here, Winston.

I do love sitting in the garden with you, laughing and gossiping.

Winston Yes.

It's all right. Not bad.

Well, a bloke can have a good old natter with his bit of fluff here and no-one takes no notice.

You go into the village pub, look, and everyone knows.

They all starts gossiping.

Like what they're gossiping about your brother.

Rosie What are they gossiping about my brother?

William Him and that Mrs Godwin.

Rosie Why?

They're only friends like you and I.

Winston Friends? And my arse.

Your brother, my dear, is right up to his bloodshot little eyeballs in a full-scale, no-holds-barred fling.

Rosie William is having a fling with Mrs Godwin?

Winston Yes.

Well, they all does sooner or later.

Hope he don't go the same way as old Wilson Rappaport.

Rosie Pardon?

Winston Old Wilson Rappaport, he had a fling with Mrs Godwin see.

That's why he committed suicide.

Rosie Suicide?

Winston Yes.

In that shed at the bottom of your garden.

Rosie What?

Winston They found him there the day before the village fête.

He done himself in.

They reckoned it was because Mrs Godwin had given him the elbow, back-heeled him look.

Hope William don't go the same way, eh, Rosie?

Rosie William and Mrs Godwin!

Who would have believed it?

After all these years. And a beautiful woman, too. An elegant woman.

What's happening?

What's happening to us, Winston?

Black-out

Fade up the Lights back on Nancy

Nancy (*to the audience*) It's Winston—that's what's happening to us.

He's destroying us.

He's eating us up.

We've got to get rid of him.

It's impossible having him round the house.

That disgusting little man with his tattoos and his stubble and his hairy navel and his...

I'm still being watched.

I'm still being laughed at.

Laughter

They're holding a committee meeting.

In our house.

About the village fête.

They're actually holding a committee meeting, and they didn't bother to tell me about it.

Fade up the Lights on the drawing room. Laughter

Present are William, Rosie, Mrs Godwin, Stanley and Janet

William Thank you, thank you.

Order if you please.

Stanley Yes, indeed.

Could we have some order please?

Laughter subsides

William Thank you, Stanley.

Well, everyone, as your chairman may I say how nice it is of you all to make yourselves available this evening.

Particularly Lucy.

Although, of course, that doesn't preclude Stanley and Janet and Rosie and Winston.

Winston Hear hear.

Now get on with it.

William Yes.

Well, we have apologies from Freddie Hayballs who can't be present owing to personal bereavement in the family.

Winston Personal bereavement?

Rubbish.

I knows all about Freddie Hayballs.

He's my first cousin.

He'll be nicking from the abattoir.

It's his night for it.

He'll be down there with old Jim Filbert and they'll be...

Rosie Winston!

Winston Sorry, Rosie.

Carry on, William.

William Thank you, Rosie.

We have another apology here from the Colonel who can't be with us owing to an outbreak of fungus on his ornamental carp.

Right then, to summarise so far.

The village fête, as you know, is just four days away, and everything seems to be in order.

The stalls have been allocated. Winston is to cut the grass on the meadow on the morning of the fête, the Salvation Army Band has been booked and the Boys Brigade will be doing their usual demonstration.

I believe it is their usual contribution, isn't it, Lucy?

Mrs Godwin That's right, William.

Their usual demonstration of the things boys get up to.

Winston Hear, hear.

And hurry up, William.

I got a heavy sesh on at the pub tonight.

I oiled my old peg board special for the crib, ain't I?

William Sorry, Winston.

Well, I've instructed the Fire Brigade to stand by and...

Father enters

Father Oh.

Not barging in on anything important, am I?

Rosie As a matter of fact, you are, Father.

We're holding a committee meeting.

Father I say—a committee meeting.

I like committee meetings.

Fearfully fond of them.

When I was in India with your mother when she was alive, we used to have any number of committee meetings.

Yes, I'll never forget them.

Can't remember what they were about, but they were most frightfully memorable.

I recall this wallah with the big ears and the spindly little hairy legs and——

Winston begins to roar with laughter

—or was it the other wallah with the cracked monocle and the arch supports and——

Rosie joins in the laughter. So do the others. Even Father. The laughter grows louder and louder

Then cross-fade to Nancy's point of hearing as she sits in her sewing room

Nancy (*to the audience*) They're laughing.

Why are they laughing?

We've never had laughter in our house before.

Never ever.

Our houses have always been noted for their lack of laughter.

What's going on?

What on earth is going wrong with this family?

What's going wrong with me?

That disgusting little man with the Zapata moustache and the stubble on his chin will be sitting in my drawing room, scuffing his boots on my carpet, dropping his cigarette ash on my sofa, spitting into the fireplace, wiping his nose on the loose covers and ... and...

I can't cope.

I can't cope. I cannot cope.

Black-out

Lights up on the kitchen next morning

Rosie is at the table eating. Winston, in a pinnie, is doing the ironing

Rosie Do you like ironing, Winston?
Winston Oh yes, Rosie, without a doubt.
Very conducive to the contemplative processes of philosophising look.
Do you reckon I should put a bit more starch in William's underpants.
Rosie (*laughing*) Oh, Winston, don't be so awful.

Nancy enters

Hallo, Nancy.
You're up early.
Nancy Yes, I thought I'd...
What on earth are you eating?
Rosie Dripping toast.
Nancy Dripping toast?
And you're drinking wine.
Rosie Port wine.
It's lovely.
You want to try it.
Put a bit of flesh on you, Nancy.
Make you rich and juicy and all desirable.
Winston That it will, Nancy. That it will.
Here.
Have a swig from the bottle.
Nancy Go away.
Go away from me, you disgusting little squirt.

She exits into the garden

William, in his pyjamas, is dancing round clutching a broom tightly to his chest

      William, what on earth are you doing?

William Dancing, Nancy.

Nancy Why?

William Because I'm happy, Nancy.

      I'm glad to be alive.

      Isn't it wonderful here?

      Isn't it lovely to live in this village being committed, being an integral part of the community, being wanted?

      That's what Lucy says, anyway, and I agree with her wholeheartedly.

Nancy William.

William Yes, Nancy?

Nancy You're not writing, are you?

William Oh yes, I am.

Nancy What are you writing?

William Mucky books.

Nancy What?

William I am writing a book about wife swappers.

Nancy Wife swappers?

William Yes.

      Wife swappers on the Manchester, Altrincham and South Junction Railway.

Nancy You bastard.

      You absolute bastard.

She runs to the bottom of the garden and bursts into the shed

Father What-o, Nancy. It's only me.

      Do you know, I have never felt better in the whole of my life.

Nancy What?

Father I feel wonderful.

Nancy But what about your legs?

      What about your chest and your sinuses and your attacks of vertigo?

Father All as sound as a bell, Nancy.

      And do you know why?

Nancy Tell me, Father.

Father Living here, old boy.

      In this village.

      In this house.

Being part of the community.

Being part of the human race, Nancy, and feeling that I'm giving to my fellow men without restraint the love and kindness and radiant warmth that I've concealed all these years deep down in my soul and ... and...

And I've stopped drinking gin.

Nancy Pardon?

Father I don't think I ever told you, Nancy, but I've always been a secret drinker.

Well, you don't want to broadcast that sort of thing, do you?

I used to hide the bottles from you.

You never found out.

I was far too clever.

I'm not pleased about it.

In fact I'm profoundly ashamed about it.

But now it's all stopped, Nancy.

No more gin drinking for me.

I'm so happy.

Yes.

So happy.

I remember we used to drink rather a lot in India.

Gin.

Your mother and I.

Good God, we drank oodles and oodles of gin.

Nancy (*almost screaming*) Father, Father, how can you?

How can you do this to me?

I can't cope with it.

I can't cope.

She races out. She races into the house and flings herself on to her bed. She begins to cry. She sobs and she sobs and she sobs

The door opens softly. Winston steps inside

Winston Not disturbing you, am I, missus?

I just wanted to look at your...

You're crying.

Nancy Go away.

Winston You're crying, Nancy.

Why are you crying?

Nancy I'm not crying.

Go away.

Winston Right then, I'll…

Nancy No.

Stay.

Winston Right.

I'll stay.

I'd lend you my hankie only it's covered in snots look.

(*He pauses*) Why was you crying, Nancy?

Nancy I don't know.

I just can't help it.

Winston You didn't ought to cry at your age, missus.

Nancy I'm not old.

Winston I knows you ain't old.

You ain't old at all, Nancy.

In fact, I thinks you look very young.

You looks very desirable if you don't mind me saying so.

Nancy What?

Winston You looks desirable.

I'm an expert on women being desirable.

Nancy Are you?

Winston Without a doubt, Nancy.

I has been all my life.

That's how I knows my wife ain't desirable.

That she ain't.

Very far from it.

But you are.

Nancy Am I?

Winston Yes, you are, Nancy.

Very desirable indeed.

(*He pauses*) You don't want a new downpipe for your outside bogs, do you?

Free and gratis.

Nancy Get out.

Get out, you disgusting man.

How dare you burst into my bedroom with your muddy boots and your bad breath and your dirty, greasy hair.

Get out.

Out, out, out. (*She sinks back on her bed sobbing*)

Winston stares at her silently for a moment

Fade out the Lights on Nancy, then follow Winston as he makes his way through the house to the garden. William stops him

William Ah, Winston, just the man.

You remember that demonstration you gave me on the art of french kissing?

Well, I'm going round to Mrs Godwin's this evening and I thought a little refresher course might not come amiss and...

Winston Get lost.

Get lost, you little maggot. (*He moves on*)

Rosie stops him

Rosie Winston! Hi!

What about a trip out in your car, your motor?

It's a lovely evening and I thought we could...

Winston No, Rosie.

Not now.

I ain't got the stomach for gallivanting look. (*He steps into the garden*)

Father shuffles over

Father Ah, Winston, caught you at long last.

I don't want to complain, old boy, but it's about my long johns.

I don't know if you're aware of it, but there's the most fearful scorchmark on the crutch.

Hang on a mo, and I'll show it you. (*He starts to undo his trousers*)

Winston Go away.

Go away, old man, and leave me in peace.

Father, deeply puzzled, shuffles off

Winston sits on the wall

(*After a pause*) That dog of mine.

He stopped barking.
Why's my dog stopped barking?

Fade out Lights on Winston

Lights up on Nancy still in her bedroom

Nancy (*to the audience*) I can't get up.
I can't step out of my bedroom.
I've been here for days.
My legs feel like lead.
There's a little pulse in my neck twitching and throbbing.
I can't move.
But I'm watching them.
Oh yes, I'm watching them.
Winston, naked to the waist, hairy belly, dusty and taut, smiling and whistling through the gap between his two front teeth.
William laughing and crowing and quite blatantly going in and out of Mrs Godwin's house.
Rosie sitting side by side with Winston and laughing and stroking his arm and pinching his cheeks and ... and...
And Winston looking at her all soft and tender.
And there's Father.
And he's smiling.
Not drinking.
Not complaining about his health.
Showing his underpants to Winston and...
Winston!
I'm not old.
I know I'm not old.
I'm young.
I'm desirable.
(*She pauses. Then softly*) I'm tasty.
I'm tasty.
Without a doubt.
(*She lies on the bed*) It's the night before the village fête.
I can't sleep.
I feel restless and...
Someone's watching me.
(*She pauses*) I know who it is.

I do. I do.
It's Wilson Rappaport.
It has to be.
He's still in this house.
Of course, he is. Of course.
He's looking at me from every nook and cranny like the spider in the house we left in London.
And everything in this house is his.
Every person in the house is his.
He's taken them over.
Rosie's laughter is his.
Father's happiness is his.
William's ardour is his.
He's taken over everyone in this house.
Everyone except me.
(*She pauses*) The owls are hooting.
The starlings are scuttering in the eaves.
What's that?
The floorboard's creaking outside my room.
Listen. Listen.
The door's opening.
Someone's coming in.
(*She is tense with horror*) It's a man.
I can hear the rasp of his breath.
I can feel his breath on my cheeks.
I can feel his hands on my body. I can feel them running over my shoulders and over my breasts.
He's climbing into bed beside me. (*She suddenly screams at the top of her voice. She leaps out of bed, dashes through the house into the garden and kicks open the door of the shed*)

There on the floor lies William

William! William!

Rosie and Father come rushing up

Rosie Nancy, whatever is the matter?
Nancy It's William.
          He's dead.

Rosie Oh, William.
>   William, William.
Father He's not dead, old boy.
>   He's drunk.
Nancy He's dead.
>   He's dead, I tell you.
Father He's drunk.
>   He's as drunk as a Lord.
>   I've seen oodles and oodles of drunks in my time.
>   Saw loads of drunks in India.
>   Oodles and oodles of them.
>   That's why we lost the Empire—drank it to death.
>   Look at him.
>   He's still breathing.
>   Smell his breath.
>   Whisky.
>   He's been drinking gallons of the stuff.
>   I'll give him a good kick in the ribs.
>   That'll sort him out.
>   There. Take that.

He kicks him violently in the ribs

William (*groaning and crying out with pain*) Oh, Lucy.
>   Lucy, Lucy.
Nancy Lucy?
>   What's Lucy got to do with it?
William She's abandoned me.
>   She's thrown me to the wolves.
>   Oh, Lucy, Lucy.
Nancy You bastard.
>   You swine.

She kicks him violently in the ribs

>   *He staggers to his feet and lurches off, pursued by a furious Nancy and
>   a giggling Rosie trying to restrain her*

>   *Father is left alone. He puffs silently at his pipe for a moment, then smiles*

Father And then on another occasion I was unfaithful.
In Calcutta.
Three times.
On the trot.
Didn't even have time for a decent pipe.

Black-out

Lights up on the garden, on the morning of the village fête

Stanley and Janet enter

Stanley Come on, sleepy heads.
Wakey wakey.
Janet It' a lovely day.
It's a perfect day for the fête.
Stanley The band's playing, everyone.
Can you hear the band?

In the background, a brass band faintly strikes up

Janet And Winston's mowing the meadow.
Can't you hear him swearing?
Stanley Come on, everyone. Show a leg.

Separately, Nancy, William, Rosie, and Father enter

Janet Isn't this exciting?
Another fête. Another new dress.
Stanley made it last night.
What do you think, everyone?
Father Very nice, old boy.
Reminds me of a garden party I once went to in Cawnpore.
There was this big marquee, you see, and...
Rosie You're smiling, William.
William Of course I'm smiling.
Why shouldn't I smile?
Rosie But Mrs Godwin.
I thought she'd abandoned you.

William She has.

Thrown me out.

But, my dear Rosie, there are plenty more fish in the sea.

Have you seen that Betty Hayballs?

Cor!

Cor!

He exits, followed by Stanley and Janet

Nancy (*softly*) I can't cope.

I can't cope.

Rosie Oh gosh, this is going to be a lovely, lovely day, Nancy.

It's going to be one of the best days of my life.

I know it is.

A whole day at the stall with Winston.

Nancy (*savagely*) Winston!

Winston!

Why you have to go round with that ghastly slob of a man I do not know.

That disgusting man with his nicotine stains and his greasy hair and his tattoos over his nipples and his dirty, slimy teeth and his…

Rosie He is not a disgusting man.

He is not a slob.

Winston is one of the finest men I have ever met.

He is a lovely, lovely man, and if he weren't married, I would scoop him up in my arms and we would run off and we would live in a caravan high in the hills and we would go wandering round leafy lanes and our life would be bliss and I'm not going to have you spoil my dreams.

You've spoiled our lives before with your bossing and your martyrdom and your coping.

Your constant bloody coping.

And I'm not going to stand for it any longer.

I can cope on my own.

Goodbye.

She marches off

Father Yes.

Yes, well, I think I'll potter off, too, old boy.

Might just call in at the pub.
Just for a quick one.
Nothing alcoholic, of course.
A Bloody Mary without the tomato juice.
Toodle pip, old bean.
Toodle pip.

He shuffles off

Nancy (*to the audience*) I want to go with them.
But I can't.
I want to join in.
But I can't.

Brass band music louder now

If I creep very softly to the bottom of the garden, I'll be able to see them.
(*She tiptoes to the bottom of the garden and looks out*) There.
There they are.
And they look so happy.

As she talks, Winston appears and walks softly up to her

They're laughing and smiling.
Why can't I laugh? Way can't I smile?
Why can't I join in?
(*She pauses*) I'm so lonely.
I'm a lonely old woman.
Winston Hallo, Nancy.
Nancy (*crying out with alarm*) Winston!
You frightened the life out of me.
Winston Yes.
That's what I done first time you met me, ain't it, Nancy?
(*He pauses*) You looks happy, missus.
Nancy Me?
Winston Yes, Nancy.
You.
Nancy (*sharply*) Why aren't you at your stall?
You're supposed to be working with Rosie, aren't you?

Winston I just slipped out to see where you was.

Nancy Why?

Winston To tell you something.

Nancy What?

Winston I'm going back home to my missus.

Nancy You're going back home?

    Why?

    Why, Winston?

Winston I just seen my missus look.

    At the fête.

    They has this stall, see, and they picks the ugliest woman in the whole of the village to lie on a bed and they gives you a ball and if you throws it and hits the target correct and proper, the bed turns turtle and tips the woman into a bloody great bath full of cold water.

    Well, my missus is the ugly woman, Nancy.

    And I seen her there lying in the bed.

    And underneath her was this whacking great bath golloping with ice cold water.

    And I thought—why not?

    Just one last throw for old time's sake.

    And I took the ball in my hand.

    I took careful aim, Nancy.

    I hurled it with all my might.

    And it landed smack on the target, and out she fell into the bath with a bloody great splash and everyone cheered and everyone roared and hollered and I thought...

    I thought, my heart's turning over.

    And I knew I could never leave her, Nancy.

    I knew that it was always ordained I should live with an ugly woman. Not with someone like you, Nancy.

    You're a beautiful woman.

    You're a tasty woman, handsome and bold and I desires you and I wants you and I loves you.

Nancy (*softly*) Winston.

Winston Lie down, Nancy.

    Lie down here on the ground beside old Winston.

He takes hold of her and gently lies her down. He joins her. He kisses her softly

I loves you, Nancy. I really loves you.

Nancy Winston, Winston.

Winston You ain't never had a man before, has you, Nancy?

Nancy I... I...

Winston You ain't never had a bloke proper in the whole of your life, has you?

Nancy No.

Winston fondles her gently

Winston Why not?

Nancy I... I've been too busy keeping the family together.
I haven't had time.
All my life has been consumed by keeping them together.

Winston Very noble, Nancy.
It's very noble to keep people together.

He draws her closer to him

To pull them together.

He draws her close into him

To snuggle them up closer together.

He hugs her. He kisses her. She sighs. Suddenly, he draws back

Nancy.

Nancy Yes, Winston?

Winston When we've done what we got to do, I've got a present for you back at the house.

Nancy Oh, Winston, what is it?

Winston A new downpipe for your outside bogs.
Free and gratis.

Nancy Oh, Winston, Winston, Winston.

She throws herself at him. Fade out the Lights as they embrace fiercely

I'm so happy. I'm so happy. I'm so happy.

As it gets to Black-out, she cries out in ecstasy

I'm so happeeeeeeeeeee!

Father enters very slowly. He wears a funny hat on his head. Round his shoulders are paper streamers. In one hand he carries a coconut. In the other he has a plastic bag with a goldfish

Father And so am I.
Fearfully happy.
Overwhelmingly, overpoweringly, thunderously happy.
(*He pauses*) Or do I mean bloody miserable?

CURTAIN

FURNITURE AND PROPERTY LIST

Further dressing may be added at the director's discretion

ACT I

On stage: Packing cases
Black plastic sacks
Sockets
Typewriter
Drawing board
Furniture with cushions
Flowers in the garden

Off stage: Rusty old lawn mower and an assortment of gardening implements
(**Removal Men**)
Large sledgehammer (**Winston**)
Newspaper (**Father**)
Sewing (**Rosie**)
Tea things (**William** and **Mrs Godwin**)

Personal: **Father:** pipe
Winston: screwdriver

ACT II

Set: Deck chair
Easel
Kitchen table and chairs
Eating utensils
Bed

Off stage: Trolley with food, crockery, and cutlery (**Winston**)
Broom (**William**)
Coconut, plastic bag with a goldfish (**Father**)

Personal: **Father:** pipe, paper streamers (later)

LIGHTING PLOT

Property fittings required: nil
2 interior and 2 exterior settings

ACT I

To open: Overall general lighting

Cue 1	**Father** exits slowly *Black-out, then bring up lights on the garden of the new house*	(Page 8)
Cue 2	**Rosie**: "Then we'd better call up Winston, hadn't we?" *Black-out, then bring up lights on* **Nancy**	(Page 15)
Cue 3	**Nancy**: "And that is our final word on the subject." *Black-out, then bring up lights as* **Father** *wanders on*	(Page 23)
Cue 4	**Father** : "Fearfully amusing, don't you think?" *Fade out on* **Father**, *then fade up lights on* **William**	(Page 23)
Cue 5	Hammering and banging starts off *Fade to black-out*	(Page 25)
Cue 6	**Nancy**: "…still tippling at his gin." *Fade up lights on Father in the garden*	(Page 26)
Cue 7	**Nancy**: "Stop watching me." *Black-out, then bring up lights on the drawing room*	(Page 28)
Cue 8	**Nancy**: "And I hate village fêtes, too." *Black-out*	(Page 32)
Cue 9	Hammering stops *Bring up lights on* **William**	(Page 32)
Cue 10	**Winston**: "…old Winston comes to pay his court." *Fade out, then fade up lights back on the drawing room*	(Page 34)

ACT II

To open: Overall general lighting

Cue 11	They all start to eat with gusto *Fade out lights, then fade them up on the garden*	(Page 46)
Cue 12	**Winston** and **Rosie** kiss *Black-out, then bring up lights on next morning in the garden*	(Page 49)
Cue 13	**Nancy**: "What's happening to us all?" *Fade out, then fade up lights on the drawing room*	(Page 50)
Cue 14	**Mrs Godwin**: "…books on railways, isn't it?" *Fade out, then fade up lights on Nancy in the garden*	(Page 53)
Cue 15	**Nancy**: "The whole world's going mad." *Cross-fade to* **Father** *smoking in the shed*	(Page 54)
Cue 16	**Father**: "On the trot." *Fade out, then fade up lights for next morning*	(Page 57)
Cue 17	**Nancy**: "…for a while in my sewing room." *Follow spot on* **Nancy** *into her sewing room*	(Page 59)
Cue 18	**Winston**: "…by the way, are you, Nancy?" *Black-out*	(Page 62)
Cue 19	Laughter *Slowly fade up lights on the scene around* **Father**	(Page 62)
Cue 20	**Rosie**: "What's happening to us, Winston?" *Black-out, then fade up lights on* **Nancy**	(Page 64)
Cue 21	**Nancy**: "…they didn't bother to tell me about it." *Fade up Lights on the drawing room*	(Page 64)
Cue 22	The laughter grows louder and louder *Cross-fade to* **Nancy** *in her sewing room*	(Page 66)
Cue 23	**Nancy**: "I cannot cope." *Black-out, then bring up lights on the kitchen next morning*	(Page 67)

Cue 24   **Winston** stares at **Nancy** silently for a moment   (Page 71)
           Fade out lights on **Nancy**, *then follow spot on* **Winston**

Cue 25   **Winston**: "Why's my dog stopped barking?"   (Page 72)
           Fade out lights on **Winston**, *then bring up lights on*
              Nancy *in her bedroom*

Cue 26   **Father**: "Didn't even have time for a decent pipe."   (Page 75)
           Black-out, then bring up lights on the garden in the
              morning

Cue 27   **Winston** and **Nancy** embrace fiercely   (Page 79)
           Fade lights to black-out

EFFECTS PLOT

ACT I

Cue 13   **Father**: "...on the back of my neck again."   (Page 35)
            Doorbell rings, then it rings again

ACT II

Cue 14   **Father** is pottering slowly round the garden   (Page 40)
            Dog barking in the distance

Cue 15   **Stanley**: "Can you hear the band?"   (Page 75)
            Brass band faintly strikes up

Cue 16   **Nancy**: "But I can't."   (Page 77)
            Brass band grows louder